TRAVEL BUCKET LISTS

SPORTS VENUE BUCKET LIST

BY TODD KORTEMEIER

CONTENT CONSULTANT
Deane Lamont, PhD
Professor of Kinesiology
Saint Mary's College of California

Core Library

An Imprint of Abdo Publishing
abdobooks.com

Cover image: Fenway Park is home to the Boston Red Sox.

abdobooks.com

Published by Abdo Publishing, a division of ABDO, PO Box 398166, Minneapolis, Minnesota 55439.

Core Library™ is a trademark and logo of Abdo Publishing.

Printed in the United States of America, North Mankato, Minnesota.
102021
012022

THIS BOOK CONTAINS
RECYCLED MATERIALS

Cover Photo: Winslow Townson/AP Images
Interior Photos: Jeff McIntosh/The Canadian Press/AP Images, 4–5, 7, 45; Red Line Editorial, 8, 24, 42–43; Shutterstock Images, 10, 16; Israel Pabon/Shutterstock Images, 12–13; Gene J. Puskar/AP Images, 18; Richard Shiro/AP Images, 20–21; Bryan Pollard/Shutterstock Images, 27; Matt Patterson/AP Images, 28–29; Nate Hovee/Shutterstock Images, 32; Grindstone Media Group/Shutterstock Images, 34–35; Charlie Riedel/AP Images, 39

Editor: Marie Pearson
Series Designer: Joshua Olson

Library of Congress Control Number: 2020948267

Publisher's Cataloging-in-Publication Data

Names: Kortemeier, Todd, author.
Title: Sports venue bucket list / by Todd Kortemeier
Description: Minneapolis, Minnesota : Abdo Publishing, 2022 | Series: Travel bucket lists | Includes online resources and index.
Identifiers: ISBN 9781532195273 (lib. bdg.) | ISBN 9781644947357 (pbk.) | ISBN 9781098215583 (ebook)
Subjects: LCSH: Travel--Juvenile literature. | Ball games--Juvenile literature. | College sports--Juvenile literature. | Stadiums--Juvenile literature. | Sports tournaments--Juvenile | Vacations--Juvenile literature.
Classification: DDC 910.20--dc23

JAPAN
RIO
VALLETTA
MALTA
SOUTH
AFRICA
AUSTRALIA
INDIA
ALASKA
RISING SUN COUNTRY
ETH

CONTENTS

CHAPTER ONE

PART OF THE ACTION

The athlete looks over her sled at the Whistler Sliding Centre in Whistler, British Columbia, Canada. She is ready to launch herself face-first down an ice-covered track at 60 miles per hour (100 km/h). It may sound like madness. But it is a real Olympic sport called skeleton. Only this isn't the Olympics. This is just another day at Whistler.

The Whistler Sliding Centre is part of Whistler Olympic Park. Whistler hosted

Canada's Michelle Kelly practices skeleton at Whistler ahead of the 2010 Olympics.

skeleton for the 2010 Winter Olympics. Today it is open to the public. It is one of the few places on Earth where the public can try skeleton.

The track is clear. The skeleton racer takes off. She tucks her arms back for as little wind resistance as possible. With her chin just inches above the ice, she leans left or right to carve through the turns. Even though her heart is racing, she has to stay relaxed. That will help her reach top speed.

ICE TRACKS

One Olympic track for bobsled, luge, and skeleton is still standing in Switzerland. The track Cresta Run in Saint Moritz hosted two Winter Games. One was in 1928, and the other was in 1948. This track is unlike any other on Earth. Winter temperatures keep the track frozen. It has to be rebuilt after it melts each summer.

After she crosses the finish line, the track slopes up to help her come to a stop. Then she sees her time. There are no medals on the line. But it is a thrilling, once-in-a-lifetime experience.

Whistler Sliding Centre also hosted other Olympic sports, including luge, where athletes slide faceup and feetfirst.

In the rest of Whistler Olympic Park, visitors can cross-country ski where Olympians once did. They can also try their hand at biathlon, a hybrid sport of skiing and shooting.

There are only a few Winter Games venues left around the world. Not all cities kept their venues intact. And even fewer are open to the public. Whistler is a place where visitors can be a part of history.

WHERE OLYMPIC DREAMS COME TRUE

In 2020 there were five former Winter Olympic venues in North America where visitors could test their skills in a variety of Olympic sports. What do you notice about their locations?

WHISTLER OLYMPIC PARK
WHISTLER, BRITISH COLUMBIA
bobsled, skeleton, biathlon

CANADA OLYMPIC PARK
CALGARY, ALBERTA
luge, bobsled

LAKE PLACID OLYMPIC CENTER
LAKE PLACID, NEW YORK
ice skating, luge

SQUAW VALLEY SKI RESORT
OLYMPIC VALLEY, CALIFORNIA
downhill skiing

UTAH OLYMPIC PARK
PARK CITY, UTAH
bobsled, ice skating, curling

CANADA
UNITED STATES
MEXICO
N
W
E
S

THE FAN EXPERIENCE

In other venues, fans can be witnesses to history. Most sports venues don't let fans play where athletes do. Instead the fans are part of the crowd, rooting their team to victory.

Camp Nou in Barcelona, Spain, is one of the largest soccer stadiums in the world. Nearly 100,000 fans pack the stadium for FC Barcelona's biggest matches. Those fans come together with one voice to cheer on their beloved Barça.

PERSPECTIVES

CHRISTIAN NICCUM

Visitors to Whistler only get to slide on a portion of the track. They don't experience the full speed that Olympians did. Luger Christian Niccum crashed on his first run on the track in 2009. At 90 miles per hour (145 km/h), the friction on a rider's suit sliding along the ice after a crash builds up intense heat. "I didn't want to go [on a second run]," Niccum said to the *Seattle Times*. "I'm thinking, 'I have a kid on the way. I don't want to do this. . . . It's the fastest track in the world. If anyone says anything different, they're crazy."

Fans pack Camp Nou to cheer on FC Barcelona.

Sports venues come in all shapes and sizes. Some are huge and can host a variety of sports. Others are smaller and designed for one specific sport. They all provide a unique experience for fans.

There are a few venues that many sports fans would love to visit. These are the most famous sports venues on the planet. A game only lasts for a few hours. Memories last a lifetime. Fans get to see where history was made. Sometimes they can even watch it be made.

STRAIGHT TO THE SOURCE

Journalist Dee Raffo described her experience riding a skeleton sled at Whistler:

> *A sack of potatoes. That's what I was told to [imitate] as I hurtled down the Whistler Sliding Centre track headfirst at up to 100 kilometers per hour [60 mph]. Think like a potato—mellow, grounded, not phased by the walls of ice and [force of gravity].*
>
> *I have never had a need for speed, so winding my way around six bends of an icy track on what looks like a dinner tray was definitely something that took me out of my comfort zone. . . . As I took my place at the top of the Maple Leaf start (a third of the way up the Olympic track) I'm glad they had used such visual analogies.*

Source: Dee Raffo. "How to Skeleton and Bobsleigh in Whistler." *Whistler Insider*, 24 Dec. 2019, whistler.com. Accessed 24 July 2020.

CONSIDER YOUR AUDIENCE

Adapt this passage for a different audience, such as your younger friends. Write a blog post conveying this same information for the new audience. How does your post differ from the original text and why?

FENWAY PARK
comcast
NESN
FRIDAY NIGHT BASEBALL
AVAYA

OUT TO THE BALL GAME

Since 1912, baseball fans have gathered at the corner of Jersey Street and Van Ness Street in Boston, Massachusetts. Rising above the street is the grandstand around home plate at Fenway Park. Generations of fans have come to see a game at one of baseball's most iconic ballparks.

Stepping through the gates at Fenway is like stepping into a time machine. It is a glimpse of what it was like to go to a ball game in the earliest days of Major League

Boston Red Sox fans enjoy catching home games at Fenway Park.

Baseball (MLB). The players have changed, and Fenway has seen some improvements over the years, but many of the ballpark's famous sites remain intact.

PERSPECTIVES

TIM WAKEFIELD

Pitcher Tim Wakefield played nearly his entire career in Boston. In 17 years with the Red Sox, he made 216 starts at Fenway Park. Wakefield enjoyed the opportunity to spend his career in such a historic place. "This is a cathedral," Wakefield said to the *Boston Globe*. "I mean, are you kidding me? This thing's 100 and something years old. Some of the greatest that ever played the game stepped foot on this field and played for the Red Sox here as well. You can feel it every time you step on the mound."

One of the first things fans see when they enter is the Green Monster. Towering 37 feet (11 m) over left field, the Green Monster is the tallest outfield fence in MLB. At the base of the wall is a scoreboard operated entirely by hand. In 2003, the team added seats on top of the Green Monster. Sitting there for a game is an experience unlike any in baseball.

Before the game, or when the Sox are out of town, fans can tour the historic park. They can also see the statues of Red Sox greats Ted Williams and Carl Yastrzemski. With such a long history, almost every great player in Red Sox history has played at Fenway.

ACROSS THE PACIFIC

Baseball is known as an American sport. But many countries around the world have embraced the game too. Baseball was introduced to Japan in 1872. Today baseball is a favorite sport in the country. Its league is one of the best in the world.

Hanshin Koshien Stadium in Japan is the home of the Hanshin Tigers. It opened in 1924. It is one of the most historic stadiums in Japan. Babe Ruth once played there in an exhibition game in 1934. It has hosted Japan's national high school tournament since the 1920s. This large, prestigious tournament has featured many future major leaguers.

Visitors to Hanshin Koshien Stadium can visit its museum to explore the history of the stadium and the Tigers.

In Japan the most dedicated fans sit in the stands along the outfield wall. They sing, chant, and wave flags and towels. Superfans at the front of each section lead the cheers. Tigers fans have these cheers memorized to honor different players and inspire their team to victory.

BIG LITTLE LEAGUES

Walk into Howard J. Lamade Stadium in South Williamsport, Pennsylvania, and it looks like any classic baseball stadium. It's just a bit smaller. Lamade Stadium is home to the Little League World Series. This tournament crowns the champion of Little League Baseball, which consists of teams of players ages ten to 12.

Unlike the 90-foot (27-m) basepaths major leaguers run, Lamade features bases 60 feet (18 m) apart. The pitcher stands 46 feet (14 m) from home plate. And the outfield fence is 225 feet (69 m) away from home plate.

A small field still means big action. The Little League World Series is a truly international event.

FIELD OF DREAMS

The 1989 movie *Field of Dreams* is a favorite of many baseball fans. Part of the movie takes place on a baseball field in the middle of an Iowa cornfield. That site is preserved today for fans of the film to visit. The former farm in Dyersville, Iowa, features the original ballfield and tours of the site. In August 2021 the New York Yankees and Chicago White Sox played a game there.

Spectators watch a Little League World Series game at Lamade Stadium.

Teams come from all over the globe to compete. The Little League World Series has been held at Lamade Stadium since the stadium opened in 1959.

Admission is free. There are no tickets and no assigned seats. When not playing, the coaches and players watch games and interact with the fans. While in South Williamsport, fans can also visit the World of Little League Museum.

The field may be smaller. The fans may cheer in a different language. But there are many exciting ways to take in a baseball game.

EXPLORE ONLINE

Chapter Two discusses the experience of going to a Japanese baseball game. The article below goes into more detail on this topic. What are some other differences between an MLB game and a game in Japan that were not discussed in this chapter?

BENTO BOXES, CHANTING, AND POLITENESS DISTINGUISH JAPANESE BASEBALL

abdocorelibrary.com/sports-venue-bucket-list

MEMORIAL STADIUM
CLEMSON
UNIVERSITY
FRANK HOWARD FIELD
0
TOL 3
1ST & 10
2:32
1ST QTR
Ball On 25
TOL 3
0

ON CAMPUS

There are sports fans in every country of the world. But college sports are particularly popular in the United States. Colleges have been playing against each other in various sports since before there were professional sports.

College football began in the 1860s, nearly 30 years before the first professional game. College basketball began in the early 1890s. The first professional game happened later in that decade. Fans have been watching

The Clemson Tigers run down the hill into the east end zone of Memorial Stadium before a game.

college sports ever since. People often become fans of a college they attended. Others support their team because it represents their community. Either way, college sports offer unique experiences.

DEATH VALLEY

Memorial Stadium is the home of the Clemson University Tigers football team in Clemson, South Carolina. Its noisy conditions make it tough for opponents to win. This situation has earned the stadium the nickname "Death Valley." The nickname comes from the desert region known as Death Valley in California. The region's extreme conditions make it hard for anything to live there.

A sign on the upper deck reminds opponents where they are. It reads, "Clemson Welcomes You To Death Valley." The Tigers have won 75 percent of their home games since the stadium opened in 1942.

Above the east end zone, a hill slopes down to the field. Atop this hill is a rock. The rock was a gift to former Tigers head coach Frank Howard. It comes from the original Death Valley in California. Before each game, Clemson players touch Howard's Rock. They then run down the hill and onto the field as the band plays the Clemson fight song. The run down the hill is one of the greatest traditions in college football. It fires up the crowd of 81,500 fans and gets them ready for a Tigers win.

PERSPECTIVES

RED PARKER

When Jimmy "Red" Parker took over as Clemson football coach in 1973, attendance and general interest in the team was down. The team had stopped the tradition of running down the hill and into the east end zone before games in 1970. To help get people excited again, Parker revived that tradition. The Tigers ran down the hill once again on October 6, 1973, to excited cheers. Clemson has done it ever since. Parker said in an interview, "In my opinion, running down the hill is one of the greatest motivators in all of college football."

THE BIG HOUSE

Michigan Stadium doesn't look that big from the outside. That is only because the

THE BIGGEST STADIUMS

Only 11 stadiums in the world can seat crowds of more than 100,000. Eight of them are college football stadiums. This list shows these stadiums from smallest to largest. Why do you think college football teams need more seating than any other world sport?

100,024 | Melbourne Cricket Ground
MELBOURNE, AUSTRALIA

100,119 | Darrell K. Royal-Texas Memorial Stadium
AUSTIN, TEXAS

101,821 | Bryant-Denny Stadium
TUSCALOOSA, ALABAMA

102,321 | Tiger Stadium
BATON ROUGE, LOUISIANA

102,455 | Neyland Stadium
KNOXVILLE, TENNESSEE

102,733 | Kyle Field
COLLEGE STATION, TEXAS

102,780 | Ohio Stadium
COLUMBUS, OHIO

106,572 | Beaver Stadium
UNIVERSITY PARK, PENNSYLVANIA

107,601 | Michigan Stadium
ANN ARBOR, MICHIGAN

110,000 | Sardar Patel Stadium
AHMEDABAD, INDIA

114,000 | Rungrado May Day Stadium
PYONGYANG, NORTH KOREA

football field is lower than the ground. This hides the fact that the stadium known as the Big House is the biggest sports stadium in the United States.

The home of the University of Michigan Wolverines is located in Ann Arbor, Michigan. More than 100,000 fans pack the stadium to watch every game. The stadium's capacity is 107,000. That is nearly as large as the entire population of Ann Arbor.

Wolverines fans have been coming to Michigan Stadium

THE PIT

To University of New Mexico basketball fans, their home is known simply as "the Pit." That is because its court sits 37 feet (11 m) below ground. The seats rise up all around the court. Even though the Pit sits low in the ground, it still has a high elevation. A sign outside the visitors' locker room informs opponents that The Pit stands approximately 1 mile (1.6 km) above sea level. Another sign warns about the dangers of altitude sickness. The New Mexico Lobos have won more than 80 percent of their home games. The Pit is also one of the loudest arenas in college basketball.

since 1927. Back then, it seated only 72,000 fans. But it has steadily grown to meet the popularity of Wolverines football.

There is no upper deck at Michigan Stadium. All the seats are in one big bowl. That makes for a clear, unobstructed view from any seat.

The high-stepping Michigan marching band performs on the field before the game and at halftime. The band plays the fight song "The Victors" to welcome the home team onto the field. Fans then settle in for a game at college football's biggest stadium.

THE CAMERON CRAZIES

College basketball venues seat far fewer fans. But those fans still make plenty of noise. Some of the most passionate college basketball fans in the country come from Duke University in Durham, North Carolina.

Fans of the Duke Blue Devils have been coming to Cameron Indoor Stadium since it opened in 1940. Cameron doesn't look much like a basketball arena from

Cameron Indoor Stadium may look like an academic building on the outside, but inside it has all the features of a modern basketball stadium.

the outside. Its gray stone exterior makes it look like any other building on the Duke campus. But inside it is one of the best places to watch a game. Cameron is small by modern arena standards. It seats fewer than 10,000 fans, so they are right on top of the action.

Duke's most passionate fans are its students. They are known as the Cameron Crazies. For them, the game begins hours and sometimes days before tipoff. Students have been lining up early to get into Cameron since the 1980s. For the biggest games, they line up several days early. They sleep in tents to keep their place in line. For fans of college sports, that sort of passion just comes naturally.

WORLD CHAMPIONS
1965
1966
1967
1996
2010
ONEIDA NATION
65
63
RODGERS
12

ON THE GRIDIRON

The National Football League (NFL) runs through February, even in frigid Green Bay, Wisconsin. This is where Lambeau Field, the home of the Green Bay Packers, is located. Fans will come out to cheer on their Packers even in freezing conditions. And the Packers have played many cold games since the stadium opened in 1957.

Until 2003 the Packers had never lost a home playoff game. They won the 1967 NFL championship in the coldest title game

The Green Bay Packers have played games in the snow at Lambeau Field.

LOS ANGELES MEMORIAL COLISEUM

Few stadiums are as important in football history as the Los Angeles Memorial Coliseum. It has been home to three different NFL teams. Those teams are the Los Angeles Rams, the Los Angeles Chargers, and the Los Angeles Raiders. It has also hosted two Super Bowls. After the Rams moved out in 2019, the stadium's lone team is the University of Southern California Trojans football team. The Coliseum has hosted two Olympic Games, with another scheduled for 2028.

in NFL history. That game is now called the Ice Bowl. It earned Lambeau the nickname the Frozen Tundra.

The Packers have had a lot of success over the years. Fans can see that history at the team's Hall of Fame at Lambeau. In the hours leading up to the game, fans tailgate outside the stadium. They grill food and eat meals in the parking lot. Once inside, every Packers touchdown features a special celebration. Players jump into the front row of the stands in what is called a Lambeau Leap. The close connection between the Packers and their fans helps make Green Bay unique in the NFL.

LOUD AND PASSIONATE

Fans at Arrowhead Stadium in Kansas City, Missouri, also love to tailgate. The Kansas City Chiefs fans arrive early to get their spot. Once in place they grill up hamburgers, hot dogs, and local favorites such as Kansas City barbecue and get ready for the game.

PERSPECTIVES

TY ROWTON

Ty Rowton is a Kansas City Chiefs superfan. Game days are a big deal for him. Parking lots at Arrowhead Stadium open at 8:30 a.m. for a noon kickoff. But Rowton lines up at 6:00 a.m. to make sure he gets a good tailgating spot when gates open. Rowton said in an interview with Visit KC that arriving that early "just kind of gets you in the mood for the game. There's a lot of camaraderie with meeting people at the game—other tailgaters. It's good to see everybody around you that you've been to the game with before."

Kansas City fans are known for their loud support. Arrowhead holds the world record for loudest stadium. Fans set that record on September 29, 2014.

Mercedes-Benz Stadium has sections of clear wall that let sunlight through.

During that Monday night game against the New England Patriots, the noise reached 142.2 decibels. That is as loud as the sound of a jet aircraft taking off.

THE MODERN STADIUM

Retractable-roof stadiums are nothing new in the NFL. But Mercedes-Benz Stadium in Atlanta, Georgia, took it to a new level when it opened for Atlanta Falcons games in 2017. The stadium's roof opens in a spiral pattern. When fully open, each retracted panel resembles a falcon's wing.

Just below the roof is a huge circular video board. It is the largest in all of professional sports. It has a total size of 63,000 square feet (5,853 sq m).

The modern NFL experience is about more than just the game. Fans on certain levels of Mercedes-Benz Stadium can gaze at the Atlanta skyline and turn back to the field the next moment. Spectators also enjoy wider seats and more restrooms than the team's old stadium provided. Fantasy football enthusiasts can keep an eye on their teams with the stadium's high-speed wireless internet.

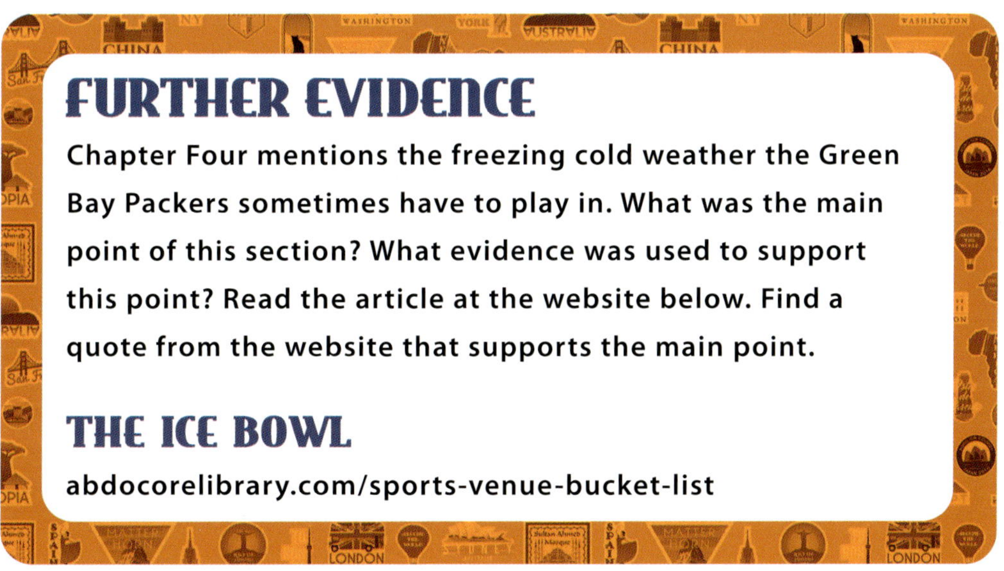

FURTHER EVIDENCE

Chapter Four mentions the freezing cold weather the Green Bay Packers sometimes have to play in. What was the main point of this section? What evidence was used to support this point? Read the article at the website below. Find a quote from the website that supports the main point.

THE ICE BOWL

abdocorelibrary.com/sports-venue-bucket-list

CHAPTER FIVE

BIG EVENTS

Among all sports venues on Earth, none are bigger than Indianapolis Motor Speedway (IMS). It is so big that it's located in its own town. Speedway, Indiana, contains IMS and not much else.

IMS has 250,000 permanent seats. With temporary seats and standing room in the infield, it can fit close to 400,000 fans. Its biggest crowds come out for the Indianapolis 500. Usually held on Memorial Day weekend,

Indianapolis Motor Speedway can seat a lot of fans.

the Indy 500 is one of the oldest and most famous auto races in the world.

MONACO GRAND PRIX

The Monaco Grand Prix is one of the top events in Formula One auto racing. It has been held since 1929 in Monaco, a small country bordered by France and the Mediterranean Sea. Each year it takes organizers six weeks to transform city streets into a racetrack. That includes 13 miles (21 km) of barriers and 215,000 square feet (20,000 sq m) of fencing. They then have to set up temporary grandstands for fans. Not all fans take a seat, though. With the track right next to the Monaco harbor, some people watch from their private boats.

The track has been improved several times since opening in 1909. But it still maintains a classic appearance. IMS is nicknamed the "Brickyard." That is because it used to be paved with brick. One yard of bricks remains at the start-finish line as a nod to history.

THE ALL ENGLAND CLUB

The All England Lawn Tennis and Croquet Club opened in 1868.

In 1877, it held its first tennis championship. The tournament was named for where the club was located in the Wimbledon neighborhood of London, United Kingdom. The Wimbledon championships have been held nearly every year since. It is a top destination for tennis fans. It is the only time the private All England Club opens its doors to the public.

The championships are unusual because they are played on real grass. That is how

PERSPECTIVES

VIV KEAN

People without tickets to Wimbledon can line up to get a seat at the biggest matches. There aren't many tickets available each day, so fans sometimes line up days in advance. They set up tents in a park across the street. Viv Kean was one of those fans at the 2019 tournament. It was not her first time. She had been to every tournament but one since 1983. She celebrated her 50th and 60th birthdays in line. And she had no plans to stop. "As long as I can get out of the tent without someone having to haul me out," Kean said to the Associated Press, "I'll continue to come."

tennis began. But today's game is usually played on a hard artificial court.

Tradition is important at Wimbledon. Players are required to wear all white clothing. Fans munch on a traditional snack of strawberries and cream. Even the British royal family sometimes comes out to watch.

AUGUSTA NATIONAL

Tradition is also a key part of one of golf's major tournaments. The Masters has been held since 1934. Unlike other golf majors, it is always at the same site. That is the Augusta National Golf Club in Augusta, Georgia.

Augusta is a private club. It has only a few hundred members and rarely accepts new ones. The only way the public can walk the grounds is to attend the Masters. And tickets are not easy to find. Masters patron badges give a person access to every day of the tournament. These badges are held for life, so there are almost never

Competitors in the Masters enjoy Augusta's beautiful course.

any available. A very small number of single-day passes are available to the public by lottery each year.

Augusta is considered one of the most beautiful golf courses in the world. Its bright green fairways and flowering azalea bushes are famous. The sand traps are filled with crushed quartz that sparkles bright white.

Some fans dream of going to Augusta for the Masters. But everyone has their own venues they want to see. Some are old classics and some are future classics. Some let fans try out a sport for themselves. Each one is somebody's idea of a can't-miss sports venue.

STRAIGHT TO THE SOURCE

NASCAR driver Tony Stewart was born and raised in Columbus, Indiana, which is near the Indianapolis Motor Speedway. In a 2014 interview, he explained his connection to IMS:

> *When you grow up 45 minutes from Indy . . . that is sacred ground to me. It always has been, always will be. I don't care how many times you win there, it's never enough. It's nice to have won two races already there. That gives you confidence of knowing what you have to do to win. It's just a matter of doing it. . . .*
>
> *It's always big when you come home. It's always big when you have friends and family that don't get the opportunity to go see you race anywhere else, but can be there and be there in person to watch and experience it with. So you're always going to run well.*

Source: "An Interview with: Tony Stewart." *Indianapolis Motor Speedway News*, 21 July 2014, indianapolismotorspeedway.com. Accessed 3 Sept. 2020.

WHAT'S THE BIG IDEA?

Stewart is using evidence to support a point. Write a paragraph describing the point Stewart is making. Then write down two or three pieces of evidence Stewart uses to make the point.

MAP

1. Whistler Olympic Park (Canada)
2. Lambeau Field (Wisconsin)
3. Arrowhead Stadium (Missouri)
4. Michigan Stadium (Michigan)
5. Indianapolis Motor Speedway (Indiana)
6. Lamade Stadium (Pennsylvania)
7. Fenway Park (Massachusetts)
8. Cameron Indoor Stadium (North Carolina)
9. Memorial Stadium (South Carolina)
10. Mercedes-Benz Stadium (Georgia)
11. Augusta National Golf Club (Georgia)
12. All England Lawn Tennis and Croquet Club (United Kingdom)
13. Camp Nou (Spain)
14. Hanshin Koshien Stadium (Japan)

GERMANY
PARIS
AUSTRALIA
RISING SUN COUNTRY
JAPAN 2016
MEXICO
EGYPT
HOLLAND
ETHIOPIA
Sultan Ahmed Mosque
14

STOP AND THINK

Surprise Me

Chapter Three discusses some notable college sports venues. After reading this book, what two or three facts about college sports venues did you find most surprising? Write a few sentences about each fact. Why did you find each fact surprising?

Dig Deeper

After reading this book, what questions do you still have about sports venues? With an adult's help, find a few reliable sources that can help you answer your questions. Write a paragraph about what you learned.

Say What?

Studying different sports venues can mean learning a lot of new vocabulary. Find five words in this book you've never heard before. Use a dictionary to find out what they mean. Then write the meanings in your own words and use each word in a new sentence.

You Are There

Chapter Two discusses attending a game at Fenway Park. Imagine you are going to a game. Write a letter home telling your friends what the game was like. What do you notice that is unique about the ballpark? Be sure to add plenty of detail to your notes.

GLOSSARY

arena
a usually indoor sports venue that is smaller than a stadium

basepath
the path between two bases on a baseball field

camaraderie
good feelings enjoyed between people

campus
the area of land on which a college is located

end zone
the area on either end of a football field where a player must bring the ball for a touchdown

grandstand
the area of a sports venue with seats for fans

iconic
very well known

spectator
a person who is watching a sport rather than playing it

tipoff
the start of a basketball game in which a member of each team tries to tip the ball back to his or her own team after it is tossed in the air

ONLINE RESOURCES

To learn more about sports venues, visit our free resource websites below.

Visit **abdocorelibrary.com** or scan this QR code for free Common Core resources for teachers and students, including vetted activities, multimedia, and booklinks, for deeper subject comprehension.

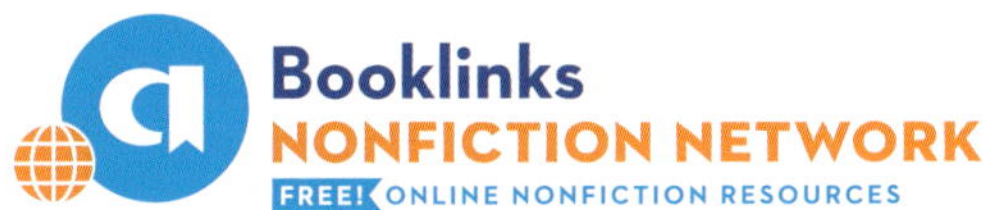

Visit **abdobooklinks.com** or scan this QR code for free additional online weblinks for further learning. These links are routinely monitored and updated to provide the most current information available.

LEARN MORE

Lowell, Barbara. *Engineering AT&T Stadium.* Abdo Publishing, 2018.

York, Andy. *Ultimate College Football Road Trip.* Abdo Publishing, 2019.

INDEX

About the Author

Todd Kortemeier is a sportswriter and sports fan who has been to 14 current MLB ballparks. He, his wife, his daughter, and their dachshund-beagle mix Ski live near Minneapolis, Minnesota.